OUR MOON

By Tara Sanderson

Library For All Ltd.

Our Moon

First published 2023

Published by Library For All Ltd
Email: info@libraryforall.org
URL: libraryforall.org

Our Yarning logo design by Jason Lee, Bidjipidji Art

Original illustrations by Michael Magpantay

Our Moon
Sanderson, Tara
ISBN: 978-1-923063-02-0
SKU03368

OUR MOON

We respect and honour Aboriginal and Torres Strait Islander Elders past, present and future. We acknowledge the stories, traditions and living cultures of Aboriginal and Torres Strait Islander peoples on this land and commit to building a brighter future together.

First there was nothing.

Then...

— the biggest BANG!

Everything exploded
and all the planets
came out.

Millions of stars burst out of the darkness.

There was a giant *crash*
when an asteroid smashed
into the new Earth.

Earth's only natural satellite, the moon, appeared.

The moon is shaped like an egg and controls the tides on the Earth.

It reflects
the light from
the Sun.

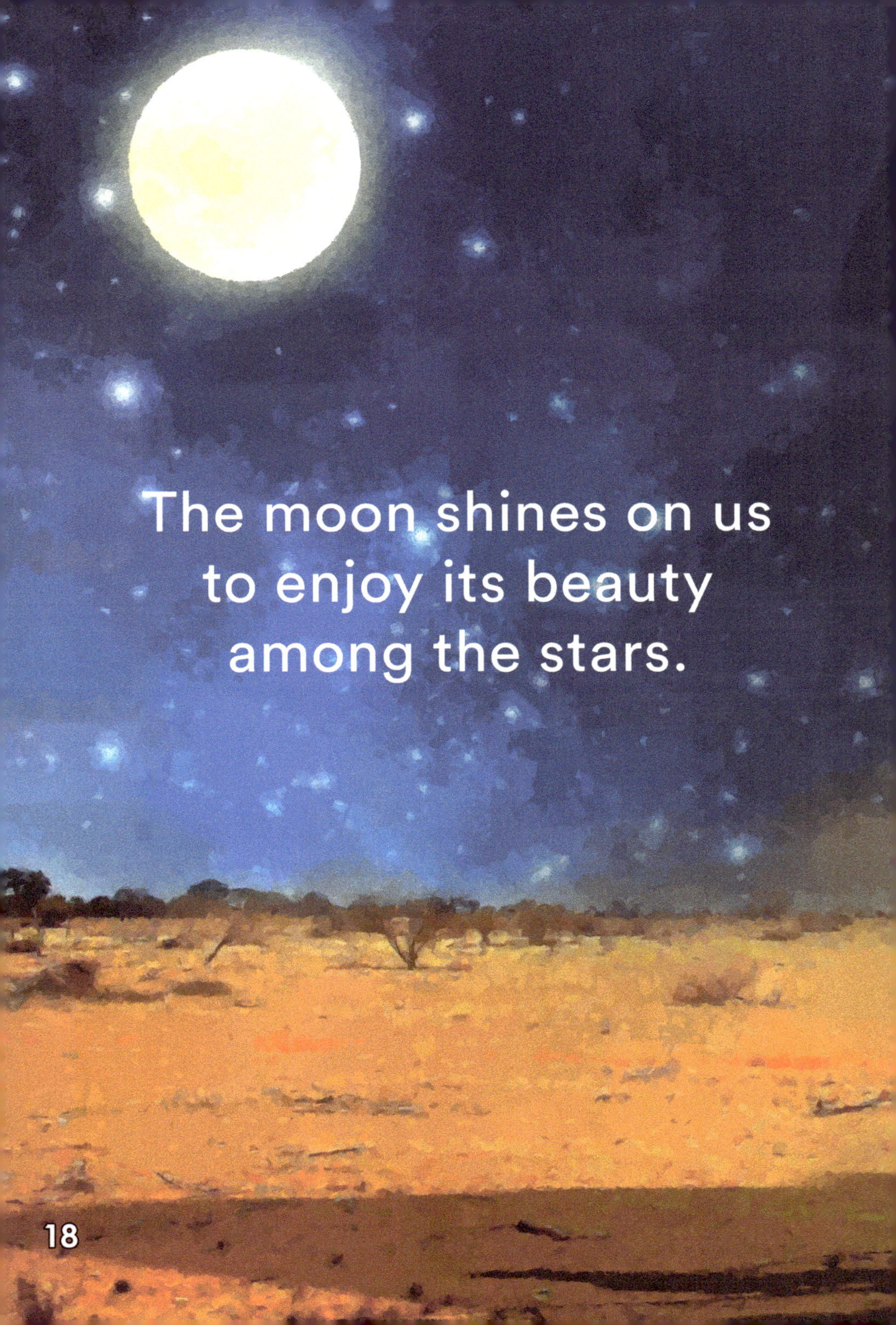

The moon shines on us
to enjoy its beauty
among the stars.

You can use these questions to talk about this book with your family, friends and teachers.

What did you learn from this book?

Describe this book in one word. Funny? Scary? Colourful? Interesting?

How did this book make you feel when you finished reading it?

What was your favourite part of this book?

download our reader app
getlibraryforall.org

About the author

Tara was born in Canberra, grew up in Queanbeyan and now lives back in Canberra. She is from the Wiradjuri Nation and loves food, family and friends. Tara's favourite story when she was little was *Wishing Tree*.

Darwin

NORTHERN
TERRITORY

QUEENSLAND

WESTERN
AUSTRALIA

SOUTH
AUSTRALIA

Brisbane

NEW SOUTH
WALES

Perth

Adelaide

Sydney

ACT
Canberra

VICTORIA

Melbourne

Author's Country

TASMANIA
Hobart

Our Yarning

Want to discover more books from this collection? Our Yarning is a collection of books written by Aboriginal and Torres Strait Islander peoples across Australia.

We know that children learn better, and enjoy reading more, when they see themselves in the stories, characters and illustrations of the books they read.

To download the app, visit the Google Play Store on any Android device and search 'Our Yarning'.